To the friends who shape our lives, and inspire us to believe.

Designed by the community supporting open-source content.

We thank you all.

www.ordinaryfinance.net

This book exists to promote knowledge.

The book is available to purchase or the content is available to download for free at:

www.ordinaryfinance.net

ISBN: 9781456591731

First published 2011 (Charleston SC)

Listed for internet distribution October 2011

This is an ordinary book.

It has been designed this way.

This is a scruffy, basic, no-frills version of other finance books that get printed.

It has been designed this way.

This book was created to make finance accessible, to make finance ordinary, to remove the mystique and fear that surrounds the topic.

It has a simple premise, a simple belief.

High finance is ordinary finance.

Most people lack confidence when dealing with financial matters.

This book is all about confidence!

BIG

FINANCE

Keep It Short

Let's start this book with an area of finance that appears so complicated, so alien to normal thinking, that showing its simplicity removes all fears for the rest of the book.

So we start with **naked short selling**, or to put it another way, selling something you do not possess.

(*During the Global Financial Crisis in 2009 many countries banned naked short selling for a period of time. It is seen by its supporters as a great way to generate profits and stimulate the world economy. Its detractors see it as something quite different.*)

Naked Short Selling

So, how do you sell something you do not own? The answer is remarkably simple.

Let's say I want to buy a new bicycle just like the one pictured below and I am willing to pay $500.

You offer to sell me a bicycle just like the one above for $500.

But as you do not possess such a bicycle, you promise to make delivery in one week.

I agree to the deal and we shake hands on it.

You now have one week to purchase an identical bicycle.

Depending on the price you have to pay, you will make a profit or a loss.

If you can purchase a bicycle for less than $500 then you will make a profit.

But if you have to pay more than $500, you make a loss.

You have taken a short position (the selling position) and I have taken a long position (the buying position).

This is called naked short selling because you do not possess the asset (bicycle) being sold, so you are deemed naked.

In real life, companies do not trade bicycles but trade assets (sometimes called securities), such as company stocks.

You can remove the "naked" by possessing the asset prior to sale.

However, possessing does not mean owning. You can simply borrow it.

I borrowed the following image from my friends Tina and Alima.

I will give the picture back, but can still sell it as part of this book.

Markets are regulated, so companies can enter into contractual agreements with confidence...

Unlike my friends, who have to simply *trust* that I will return the picture.

Short Selling (Non-Naked)

Legally you can sell assets you have only borrowed from someone. You can borrow these from a broker.

This sounds strange, but is a simple idea based on an asset being "fungible." This simply means the asset can be substituted.

Currencies are "fungible," in that one $100 note is just like any other $100 note, so it can be substituted without consequence.

If I borrow $50 from you and pay you back using a different $50 note, you do not care, because they possess the same value.

They are identical and have no emotional value (unlike my beloved bicycle).

This is also true for company shares, which—like currencies—are just paper certificates.

First, let's look at the fungibility of **currencies.**

You borrow $500 from me and promise to pay the money back in one week. You can now use the $500 to try to make a profit.

You could sell the $500 in exchange for $500 worth of company shares.

If the company share price increases 10 per cent, you could sell the shares for $550.

This will allow you to return my $500 and make a $50 profit.

If the company share price falls, you will make a loss.

Profit or Loss, at the end of the week I want my $500 back (just not necessarily the same $500).

As shares (like currencies) are also "fungible," you can substitute shares for currencies in the above example.

So let's look at **company shares.**

I lend you $500 worth of company shares (certificates), and you promise to give them back in one week.

You could sell the shares in exchange for $500 of currency.

If the company share price falls by 10 per cent, you can now buy the shares back for $450.

This will allow you to return the shares to me and make a $50 profit.

If the company share price rises by 10 per cent, you will have to pay $550 to purchase the shares back and make a $50 loss.

Profit or Loss, at the end of the week I want my shares back.

Short-Selling Loss Potential

Problems can arise with **short selling** due to the potential for unlimited losses.

For this example, let's take the traded commodity of oil.

I agree to short-sell you ten barrels of oil for $500 (a unit price of $50 a barrel).

As I do not currently possess any barrels of oil (I am **naked**), we agree a **future** date for delivery.

Now we have a **futures** contract, with a fixed price ($500) in which I am the seller so I have a (**naked**) **short** position.

To fulfil my promise, I need to purchase ten barrels of oil.

Suddenly and unexpectedly...

War breaks out in the Middle East, or a major oil spill occurs in the Gulf of Mexico.

This reduces the supply of oil, so the price increases.

(Price is related to the availability of a product; scarcity of supply results in price increases.)

Let's assumes the price of oil reaches $100 a barrel.

To fulfil our contract, I now have to spend $1,000 (10 barrels at $100 a barrel) and will make a loss of $500 (as I have agreed to a sales price of just $500).

This is the potential downside of short selling, whilst the maximum profit is capped at the sales price we agreed on in our **futures** contract ($500), the purchase price is unknown, and anything unknown has unlimited potential.

When interest rates are low,

debt is cheap.

When interest rates rise, debt is *no longer* cheap.

Be *very careful* with debt. It may not be *affordable tomorrow*.

Profit and Debt

If you make losses, you may end up in **debt**. The good news is, even debt has value and can be sold for profit. Strange but true.

This is a simple concept to follow for anyone who has held a mortgage.

Let's say I have a variable-rate mortgage and believe mortgage interest rates will rise. If interest rates do rise, my repayments will also rise, because variable-rate mortgage repayments vary according to interest rates.

You, on the other hand, believe interest rates will fall, so you believe my mortgage repayments will also fall.

This difference of opinion is the basis of how we could profit from debt.

You offer to pay my mortgage every month, if in return I promise to pay you a fixed amount equal to my current mortgage repayments.

(In effect, this means I have a fixed-rate mortgage because my payments to you are always the same, and you have a variable rate debt—my variable-rate mortgage—offset by a fixed-rate income from my payments I make to you.)

Now, if I believe interest rates will rise, then I expect my mortgage repayments to rise, so fixing my repayments sounds very attractive to me.

You, on the other hand, believe interest rates will fall, so you expect to profit. This is a difficult concept, so let's have a closer look at how it works.

For example, my mortgage is $100 a month, and I expect interest rates to rise. Let's say I expect my repayments to rise to $110 a month.

You think interest rates will fall by the same value, and so you believe my repayments will fall to $90 a month.

In our contract, I promise to pay you $100 a month in return for you paying for my mortgage repayments. If interest rates rise, I have saved myself the $10 a month increase in cost, and you will have to pay $110 to my mortgage lender, giving you a $10-per-month loss.

If interest rates fall, I am stuck paying you $100 a month, and you only have to pay my mortgage lender $90 a month, so you make a profit. One of us will make $10 a month in profit and one of us will make $10 a month loss. This is known as a "zero sum game."

The problem here is, someone is going to make a loss, and we would like to minimise losses. One way to achieve this is through **hedging and options.**

In the good times, companies look to maximise profits.

In the bad times companies look to minimise losses.

In the good times, people spend most of what they earn.

In the bad times, people wish they had money to save.

Remember the bad times!

Hedging and Options

The problem so far is the potential for us to make losses (instead of profits). Is there another **option?**

Options are one way of reducing potential losses, or to put it another way, you can **hedge** (your bets) against potential losses.

A gambler hedges when he bets "each way" on a horse race. He may think he can pick the winner, but hedges his bets by including second or third place in his bet.

To fully understand this, let's look at the world of sports.

Suppose I am a football (soccer) scout. I see a young player who looks promising (maybe the talented Luke Moore of the *The Football Ramble* fame.)

Based on my recommendation, a major Spanish football club takes out an option to buy the player for $1 million.

They pay $100,000 now and at any point can pay an extra $900,000 to purchase the player's contract outright.

If the player shows good potential, other clubs may look to buy him, and his value increases. Let's say another club is looking at offering $2 million for him.

The major Spanish football club could now exercise the option, making the remaining $900,000 payment and then sell the player for $2 million, making a $1 million profit.

If the player fails to develop, the club simply does not pay the $900,000 remaining balance and lets the option expire. The loss is then limited to the $100,000 paid in advance (the option price).

This type of option happens all the time in sports. Many large football clubs have existing options on players.

Now that we understand options, we can combine this with our short sale, so *back to my bicycle.*

You promised to sell me an identical bicycle for $500. Because you did not own such a bicycle, you agreed to make delivery in one week.

You are confident you can buy a bicycle for less than $500, but not wanting to take a large risk, you **hedge** your bets by taking out an **option**.

So you find someone who sells bicycles, and offer her $50 for the **future option** of buying an identical bicycle for $500. This means the maximum you pay for the bicycle is $550: the $50 upfront payment you just made plus the purchase price of $500.

If bicycle prices fall to $300, you simply do not take up the **option** of purchasing the bicycle. The bicycle seller keeps the bike and has made $50 for no effort.

On the other hand, you have made a gain of $200 by buying the bicycle for $300 and selling it to me for $500. You also made a loss of $50—the price of the **option.** In total, you have made a $150 net profit.

However, if prices had risen by $200, so the bicycle could only be bought for $700, you have the **option** of buying the bicycle for $500; all it cost you was the $50 option price. This **option** has limited your losses to just $50.

The same principle can be applied to almost any financial transaction. Simple, but clever!

The movement in price is often referred to as volatility. The greater the volatility, the greater the potential for profit or loss. Profiting from volatility requires an ability to accurately forecast future changes in price. To do this, we need to identify **trends** in price movement.

Pricing Trends

We now understand how we can profit by movements in price.

To forecast how prices will move in the future, we need to identify a **trend**.

The question we need to answer is, how can we spot a future price **trend?**

The price for anything is generally linked to the availability of money.

- If people have less money, they spend less, and prices fall.

- If people have more money, they spend more, and prices rise.

The major tool used for controlling the availability of money is interest rates.

Interest rates are set by central banks or government treasury departments. Simply, they are the rates charged to banks for overnight borrowing of money. If the bank's cost of borrowing increases, rest assured your cost of borrowing will also increase.

If interest rates rise, borrowing becomes more expensive. As a result, items like credit card debts and loans become more expensive, consumer spending decreases, and prices fall.

If interest rates fall, credit becomes cheap, and spending is likely to increase—resulting in price rises.

The question is, how do interest rates move and how does this impact price?

Well, interest rates generally follow a **trend**.

If you are in charge of monetary policy, you need to appear in control, with a clear strategy to ensure people maintain confidence in you.

As a result, interest rates do not fluctuate violently but follow a steady pattern.

The consequence are…

If interest rates rise, they are likely to keep rising until they stop. At that point, they start to fall, and continue to fall until they stop.

Or, to put it another way, interest rates do not rise one month, fall the next, and then keep rising and falling from month to month.

They rise steadily over time and then decline steadily over time in a continuous cycle.

That's because it makes policymakers look competent.

If you see interest rates that look like this...

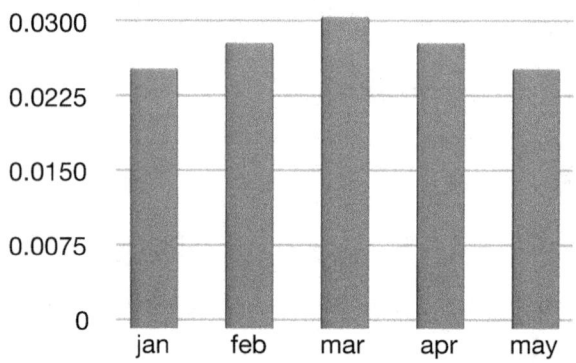

...it gives you confidence; it looks stable and gives the impression that financial policymakers are in control.

Can you imagine the reaction if interest rates did this?

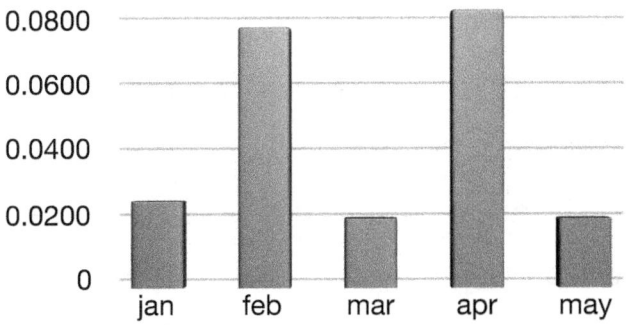

As a result, we can spot long-term trends in price reasonably accurately at a macro level through interest rate forecasts, which are somewhat predictable.

The problem is, from day to day, prices can fluctuate based on individual trades, so short-term losses and "bubbles" occur, even if interest rates are predictable.

In some cases, like the global financial crisis, the complexity of financial products masks the inherent risk (such as the risk of making a loss on a product). As a result, sudden changes to interest rates can cause large, unexpected losses.

The huge losses seen in the global financial crisis were caused by bad debt—that is, debt that no one can afford to repay.

Simple financial debts were packaged into complex products, which most people could not understand (that is, they couldn't calculate underlying risk).

Instead of this reducing prices (due to increased risk of the unknown), the debt was sold for profit and the resulting profit meant people ignored the risk. Suddenly risk was seen as a profit-making enterprise instead of a loss-minimising activity.

When interest rates were raised, the cost of debt increased, and bad debts resulted as people defaulted on loans they could no longer afford.

The resulting bad debt destabilised the global financial system and wiped out the value of many **company shares**.

Greed is not good.

Greed drives us to impress others.

Desire to achieve is good.

It drives us to conquer mountains.

The Lesson...

Aim to achieve

It will make you

smile

Company Shares

People have a lot of confusion about company shares (called *stocks* in the United States) and how they work.

In reality, **company shares** are a very old concept—because of this, they are based around common sense, so you don't have to learn complicated mathematic principles.

Let's say I have an idea for a company.

For the company to start trading, it needs money. So I lend the company money.

In return, I get a share of the company, which basically means I own a share of all its assets, liabilities, and profits.

If I am the only investor, I am likely to own 100 per cent of the shares.

But I may decide I need more investment to grow the business.

I could take a loan out and pay it back via monthly instalments, but this can be expensive. And repaying the loan takes cash out of my business each month, which I would prefer to reinvest in the business.

Instead I could offer investors a share (percentage) of the company in return for a cash investment.

As a shareholder (also called an investor) in the company, you are entitled to a percentage of the profits at the end of the year.

This is paid out in cash and is known as a **dividend**.

A company could want a wider pool of potential investors and decide to "publicly list" shares for sale.

These shares become available for others to buy and then sell on what is known as a stock exchange. (FTSE and NASDAQ are examples of stock exchanges.)

A stock exchange is just a market (like your local food market) where people buy shares (instead of food).

Investors choose which shares to buy based on an estimate of a company's future earnings and asset values.

If a company has $100 of assets and in its lifetime is expected to earn a $100 profit, it would be valued at $200. This is known as the company's **market capitalization.**

This is logical because the company can only generate $200 of value ($100 profit + selling the assets for $100). To value the company any higher would cause a loss for investors.

If we divide the **market capitalization** by the number of shares, we get the company share price.

Simple!

Company Dividends

Most companies pay shareholders a dividend every year.

This is to give investors some sort of return on the money they invested.

If a company is doing well, investors may not want to sell shares because the share price may keep rising.

But investors may like to receive some reward for investing and benefit from the company's success.

This reward is given as a dividend.

Dividends are generally paid out at the end of the financial year or halfway through the financial year.

A company's financial year and the calendar year are not necessarily the same.

If a company starts trading in June, it has a financial year from June to May, with June being the start of its financial year.

Dividends are calculated as a value per share, so a company announces it will pay a certain dollar amount per share.

If a company says it will pay out $1 per share and you have ten shares, you will receive $10 in dividend payments.

These will be taxed as a form of income.

Many large corporate investors do not want to pay tax on a dividend but prefer to gain from the increase in share price. That's because share price gains are tax free until the shares are sold.

Dividends also reduce the potential returns a company makes.

A company uses the investment from shareholders to generate profits.

Every time it has to give money back to the shareholders, the money available to invest and generate new profits reduces, thus limiting the potential to generate future returns.

As an investor, you could receive, say, a 10 per cent dividend payment from the company you invest in.

But what will you do with it?

If you put it in the bank, you will earn a much lower return, so you may want the dividend kept in the company to generate even more returns.

But then, you may only want the 10 per cent in cash if you need the cash to purchase something or to pay back a loan.

NATIONAL FINANCE

Gross Domestic Product

Countries have a financial value like companies do, and the value of the country has a very big impact on the people of a country.

If you are born into a country that has little value, your local currency will not be worth very much (compared to other currencies), and pleasures like foreign travel may not be affordable.

Many countries have value from natural resources like gold, oil, and gas.

Other countries produce value from fertile land as they produce crops and livestock. All of these assets are only valuable if the asset can be sold.

Gross Domestic Product (often called GDP) is a term used to describe the value of a nation's output (production). For example, if a country produces and sells $1 million worth of oil, the Gross Domestic Product will be $1 million.

A common indicator of national wealth is GDP per capita—that is, GDP per person. If a country earns a GDP of $1 million and has 1 million people, the population is only producing and earning a dollar per person. So GDP per capita is a strong measure of economic prosperity, with wealthy nations having a high GDP per capita.

But GDP is not the full story. A country's real value is more than the GDP.

We also need to look at how much a country spends on goods from other countries. This is called the **national trade balance** (for many countries, it is a **trade deficit**).

National Trade Balance

Our example country produces $1 million worth of milk through farming, thanks to its fertile soil.

Let's say we sell all of our milk overseas (as an export) for $1 million.

The money earned can be spent on other goods. In our example, the $1 million earned is spent on gold jewellery, which is imported from another country.

We now have an equal trade balance: we bought $1 million of jewellery *from* another country and sold $1 million of milk *to* another country.

But maybe in our country we have low interest rates and people use credit cards to purchase twice as much gold.

Now we have produced $1 million of milk sales. But we have spent twice as much ($2 million) on gold, thanks to easy credit terms.

Our trade balance is now in deficit by $1 million.

Q) But what does this mean?

A) Our country must find $1 million to pay off the trade deficit.

At some point, all trade balances must be paid, so having a large **trade deficit** is akin to spending more than you earn.

In the United States, national trade deficit in early 2010 was running at over $40 billion dollars a month.

This is a scary number, but many economists do not believe it is very important.

Some experts say high exports increase the value of a currency, so at some point the price of goods becomes too expensive to export and the balance of trade naturally corrects itself.

This view sees trade balances as a simple timing issue.

Some claim that a **trade deficit** is a good thing, because in return for assets like gold or milk, you simply give another country a piece of paper (money), which is cheap to manufacture.

The problem with a long-term deficit is your own paper (money) becomes less valuable, because you need to print more of it to pay for the imports. And so other countries become richer by comparison due to your currency being worth less (devalued).

As one of the world's richest men, Warren Buffett, said, "The U.S. trade deficit is the single biggest threat to the U.S. economy. It means other countries own more of us than we do of them."

I am not a Nobel Prize-winning economist, but I do listen to those who are older and wiser than me.

Mr. Buffett is respected for being both.

In 2009 the world's finances were dealt a shockwave thanks to the Global Financial Crisis (GFC). In the middle of this, a new term came to people's attention as governments looked to cure the potential economic problems. That term is...

Quantitative Easing

During the global financial crisis, many banks were bailed out using government funds.

The method of funding was given a new name: **quantitative easing**.

Q) What is **quantitative easing**?

A) Printing money.

Governments printed additional money to fund the banks.

This decreased the value of the currencies involved because when something becomes more abundant, it has less value.

This is why money does not grow on trees—it would have no value.

Look after your money.

It does not grow on trees!

Quantitative Easing Uses

So, after printing this extra money, what did governments do with it?

They bought bonds. But what is a bond?

A bond is simply a debt where money is loaned for a fixed term (length of time) with a fixed interest rate and a fixed price. At the end of the term, the debt must be repaid.

For example, I issue a $100 bond to raise money. The bond promises to repay $100 in eleven months. It also agrees to pay 1 per cent interest on the $100 debt each month.

Anyone who purchases the bond should receive $100 plus eleven monthly repayments (known as coupons) of $1. So the bond owner (buyer) receives $111 over eleven months, in return for giving me $100 today.

Bonds are often used to raise money [capital] instead of issuing stock. Government bonds are considered low risk, because the government can always repay the bond by printing more money—**quantitative easing**.

Bonds are openly traded on the bond market, so the price can vary. This means they do contain an element of risk.

During the global financial crisis, many governments offered to buy bonds from large banks as a form of corporate bail out.

In return for issuing new corporate bonds, banks received immediate capital in the form of cash.

This meant more cash was available to lend to both individuals and companies to stimulate spending and help improve the economy.

By having more capital, banks foreclosed on fewer businesses and repossessed fewer properties than they would have without the additional funding.

As a result, bad debts were limited, and additional credit was created to stimulate spending (demand), which in turn helped companies continue to trade (supply).

National Resources

A friend of mine living in Ghana told me Ghana had found oil, but he thought the country should keep it instead of letting companies drill for it.

"It is ours, so why should we let others get rich from it" was his thinking.

I want to talk about this in order to show why Ghana should sell its oil, and how it will benefit the country.

If the country keeps the oil, it either (1) stays under the ocean or (2) is drilled and sold to people living in Ghana.

The first option generates no income, and the second option is cost neutral because the country simply swaps oil for paper (money), which it already owns. Nothing new comes into the country, so the national economy does not benefit.

A better way must exist.

Ghana could sell drilling rights to an oil company that would be entitled to extract the oil and store it in its own oil tanks. In that case, the oil company would give money to the Ghanaian government (foreign investment) for every barrel drilled. Any foreign workers the oil company employs would need to live in Ghana and spend money locally, which would boost the Ghanaian economy.

In addition, many of the people employed for the drilling work could be Ghanaian. These people would be paid by the oil company, so new money would enter the economy. In addition, they would learn new skills.

When the oil company sells the oil, it will make a profit. Ghana can tax the company on this profit, which generates even more money for the government purse.

The government can invest this new money in local infrastructure to improve the distribution of oil through better roads, railways and seaports.

Work on the local infrastructure would employ local people, who earn a salary that they would then spend on goods and services. Local entrepreneurs would start new businesses to provide goods and services for people working on the roads, railways, and seaports.

The foreign workers would find new local products they couldn't get at home. They would tell friends, and the entrepreneurs would get orders to export goods abroad.

This would generate more money into the economy. So by selling the oil, Ghana could become rich, and my friend might start taking holidays in New York.

ALCHEMY AND FINANCE

Financial Alchemy

Every major city I go to looks like a building site. But why do cities invest in major construction projects?

The answer lies in financial alchemy.

A city invests in a major property construction programme for, let's say, $1 billion (as I said, a *major* investment property program).

Most of the $1 billion is spent on building firms and architects to construct the buildings.

The building firms now have $1 billion of revenue to pay wages and invest in future business development.

The city taxes both the firms' earnings and the employees' salaries.

So a percentage of the money invested by the city comes back to the city in the form of tax revenue. When the buildings are completed, the city will have spent $1 billion.

Companies within the city gain through additional revenue. City employees gain through the jobs created both directly and indirectly from the construction programme.

Once the project is completed, the city can sell the buildings—for, let's say, $1 billion—and all of its capital investment is returned.

The city has earned from taxes charged to the building companies and its employees, and then gets all its investment money back by selling the property.

The net effect is **financial alchemy.**

SMALL

FINANCE

Compounding

This is a very important factor in managing your personal finances.

It tells us to **start early.**

Everything in this picture started with one snowflake. But as Katie knows, lots of snowflakes mean much more fun.

How does **compounding** help us?

Money acts like snowflakes, in that it sticks to itself. It does this by attracting interest—both savings and credit attract interest.

Let's open a savings account and assume I have $100 saved on day one.

My bank offers me 1 per cent interest a day (very good terms, I know). It calculates this every two days. So in two days, I have earned 2 per cent interest (1 per cent a day over two days).

I now have $102, so I have earned $2 by saving money with a bank.

But what would happen if my bank changed the terms?

My bank offers me 1 per cent interest a day, and they calculate this *every day*.

In one day, I gain $1 (1 per cent) in interest, which gets added onto my savings account.

At the start of day two I have $101 ($100 savings plus $1 interest earned). On day two, I also earn 1 per cent interest. But this is calculated on the new balance of $101. So in day two, I earn 1 per cent of $101, which is $1.01.

So at the end of day two I have $102.01 (one cent more than the previous example). The $102.01 equals my $100 savings plus $1.00 earned day one, and $1.01 earned on day two.

By calculating and applying my interest payments daily, I have earned more money.

This is compounding.

Implications

Compounding gives us three lessons for our personal finance:

1. When saving, have the interest calculated as frequently as possible.

2. When taking on debt, have the interest calculated as infrequently as possible.

And the most important lesson:

3. Start early.

If I invest $100 a year for ten years at 5 per cent interest, I will have $1,320.68 at the end of the ten years.

My $1,000 invested earned $320.68 interest.

My 5 per cent interest gave me a 32 per cent return (**yield**).

All because I started early.

I attach the calculations on the following page.

In this example I invest another $100 of capital every year, so in year two my capital equals the year-one value plus $100 in new capital invested.

Year	Capital	Interest Rate	Value
year 1	$100.00	5%	$105.00
year 2	$205.00	5%	$215.25
year 3	$315.25	5%	$331.01
year 4	$431.01	5%	$452.56
year 5	$552.56	5%	$580.19
year 6	$680.19	5%	$714.20
year 7	$814.20	5%	$854.91
year 8	$954.91	5%	$1,002.66
year 9	$1,102.66	5%	$1,157.79
year 10	$1,257.79	5%	$1,320.68

In fact, that first $100 is worth $162.89 after ten years.

This means my 5 per cent a year interest rate has given me a 62.89 per cent return on my first $100 invested.

Again, here are the calculations, just for proof:

Year	Capital	Interest Rate	Value
year 1	$100.00	5%	$105.00
year 2	$105.00	5%	$110.25
year 3	$110.25	5%	$115.76
year 4	$115.76	5%	$121.55
year 5	$121.55	5%	$127.63
year 6	$127.63	5%	$134.01
year 7	$134.01	5%	$140.71
year 8	$140.71	5%	$147.75
year 9	$147.75	5%	$155.13
year 10	$155.13	5%	$162.89

So, as we said, **start early.**

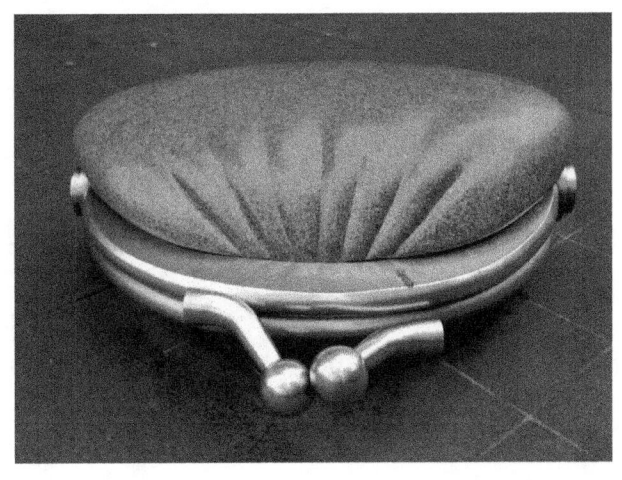

Save money and it will attract more money through interest payments. Soon you will possess a lot of money.

Mortgages

Most people at some point take out a mortgage to purchase a property. Unfortunately, most people I know do not understand the basics to enable them to choose the right mortgage for them.

Basically mortgages fall into two main types: interest-only and repayment.

Interest-Only Mortgage.

With this type of mortgage, you pay a fee every month as part of an investment fund.

None of the money is used to pay back the mortgage debt. Instead the money is invested, and every monthly payment you make adds to the investment pool.

At the end of the mortgage term, the mortgage must be repaid.

The investment fund is then used to pay back the mortgage. If the investment fund has a higher net worth than the mortgage, the mortgage is written off and the difference is paid to you in cash.

If the fund is worth less than the mortgage, you owe—and must pay—the difference.

Many people choose this type of mortgage because it is cheaper than a repayment mortgage.

But nothing is for free in life, and the price you pay for a lower monthly payment does not give you certainty about the future value of the fund.

This means you could wake up in twenty-five years and a new global financial crisis has wiped out the investment fund's profits. But you still owe the full mortgage.

It is a gamble, and gamblers win and lose.

Repayment Mortgage

With this type of mortgage, your payment is made up of two parts:

- One part is the money allocated to reduce the actual mortgage amount and is known as the capital element.

- The second part covers the interest on the mortgage.

However, you will see just one value on your monthly bank statement.

The interest is set by the bank and is based on your country's national interest rates, often set by the central bank.

The national rate just states the wholesale rate the banks can borrow at.

Your mortgage lender charges you a higher interest rate so it can make a profit from loaning you the money.

The way these mortgages are structured, you are just paying back interest in the early years.

As a result, if you switch mortgages in the early years, you see very little reduction in the outstanding debt value.

You can choose the type of interest you wish to pay, but generally it will be either fixed or variable.

A fixed mortgage rate is an interest rate that is does not change for a period of time, usually two to five years.

At the end of the fixed term, the interest rate defaults to a variable rate.

Variable mortgage rates vary according to the national interest rate.

So, if the central bank or government increases interest rates, your mortgage payments increase too.

Neither mortgage is better than the other; it comes down to a personal choice.

If you don't like risk or believe interest rates will rise, then go for a fixed rate mortgage.

If you believe interest rates will fall, then maybe a variable rate may reduce your future payments.

Subprime Mortgages

Most people first heard this term around 2008, when it was used to describe a form of lending.

Later it was blamed for the global financial crisis. But what exactly is "subprime"?

We know a mortgage is a form of debt—someone lends money to somebody else and wants it paid back (preferably with interest).

Subprime just means a lower standard of debt—that is, debt that is less likely to be paid back.

When interest rates were low, debt was cheap and people could afford to repay a higher debt value. That's why they took out bigger loans and spent more on credit cards.

Then interest rates started to rise, and these same debts became more expensive. Many people could no longer afford the repayments.

So "subprime" just means debts (such as mortgages) that are less likely to be paid back than a normal debt. The sheer volume of subprime debt meant billions were wiped off company valuations as money was not repaid.

The question is, could lenders have known that the debt was not going to be paid back before they loaned the money?

Well, in theory, yes. Investors track the "risk profile" of organisations and people so they can make accurate decisions about whether to risk lending or investing money.

If the debt is risky, people get charged a higher interest rate. The interest rate is a reward to the lender for taking a risk. This reward is known as a yield. Yields are tracked by something known as a yield curve.

Yield Curves

Yield curves show how the cost of borrowing money changes over a period of time, which is potentially important for mortgage lenders.

The yield is just the rate of return on an investment.

If I have money in a bank account, I can earn interest. This interest is the yield on the money in my bank account. If my bank account offers me 5 per cent interest a year, my bank account has a 5 per cent yield.

It is the price the bank pays me for giving them my hard-earned money. They borrow my money and promise to pay me back with interest.

Generally a yield is expected to rise over time. In other words, over time I want a greater return on my investment.

If I put money into a bank account and promise not to touch it for five years, my bank will likely offer me a higher rate of interest, which gives me a greater return (yield) on my savings.

As a result, yield curves—the cost of borrowing—tend to rise over time.

This is a function of risk.

Risk is perceived to increase over time.

If I lend you $10 today and you offer to pay me back tomorrow, there is little perceived risk.

However, if you ask to pay me back in ten years, I will ask for more than $10 back.

Over ten years, your ability to repay me may change due to poor health, lack of employment, or other factors.

In addition, the value of money may change as inflation makes products more expensive.

As a result, I will generally want a higher rate of return (yield) as time increases.

Sometimes yield curves do fall over time. This is when investors believe interest rates will fall in the future, so the cost of borrowing will decrease in the long term.

Consequently, investors are willing to accept a lower return on any investment.

How does this relate to you?

Well, let's look at a mortgage.

If interest rates today are set at 5 per cent, my mortgage lender may charge me 8 per cent interest so it can make a 3 per cent profit (return) on the debt.

However, if interest rates fall to 1 percent, a mortgage lender can charge me just 4 per cent interest and still make a 3 per cent profit (return).

The cost of borrowing in this example moved from 8 per cent to 4 per cent.

So, knowing the future yield of a debt or investment helps me to see what investors expect to happen to interest rates.

In this way, yields can help guide me when making debt or investment decisions.

You can look up yield curves on the internet for free.

Own Assets...

Buy and Lease, Instead of Paying to Rent to Someone Else.

Do not invest your money in things you do not understand.

Purchasing all these bicycles cost money.

They are an Investment.

The initial purchase is called a capital outlay.

Passers by can rent these bicycles and the money charged is given back to the investor as a **Return on Investment.**

This single investment will deliver a return for many years.

Over time, the returns should more than payback the original capital outlay.

The Lesson...

Invest in your money, and it will invest in you.

Recycling Makes Sense.

What we recycle today can be used again tomorrow.

The same principle applies to your money.

Spend it on things that give you a return on investment.

That way you can spend the money again.

The lesson...

Recycle Your Money.

A FINANCIAL TH3ORY

Efficient Market Hypothesis (EMH)

This theory is probably the most quoted financial principle in the Western world. It has a simple premise: price is a reflection of the information available, and financial markets are an accurate guide on which to base decision making.

Or, to put it another way the free financial market always reflects the most accurate price, based on the information available.

That's another way of saying the financial markets always reflect the most accurate price of company shares and other investments based on the information known to them.

If this theory were true, we would not have suffered the global financial crisis when prices crashed overnight. After all, everyone knew lenders were selling subprime debt, so that information should have been accurately priced.

Technically EMH has three versions.

Weak. Financial market prices reflect all historical information available. **As a result, they are always correct at a point in time.**

Semi-strong. Not only do financial markets reflect historical information, they also instantly change when new information is available. **As a result, they are always correct and cannot be blamed if new information changes a valuation.**

Strong. Financial markets reflect all known information and unknown information. **As a result, they are always correct, no matter what.**

You do not have to be a financial genius to realise this theory basically says, **"Trust the financial markets they are always correct."**

So, how does this theory work?

You are at a car auction, bidding for a car. Two car experts are also at the auction and are looking to gain from buying a cheap car that they can sell for a profit.

You start off bidding low in the hope of getting a bargain.

The two car experts realise the car is undervalued and, spotting a bargain, they bid higher. In theory, this will continue until your bid price reaches market price, at which point the experts stop bidding as the opportunity for profit has gone.

As a result, you pay market price because we have at least *two experts* taking part.

If you stop bidding early, the two experts will still bid against each other until it reaches market price. At this point, they will stop bidding because there is no longer a potential for profits.

Now, put this way, EMH seems to be a workable theory.

Here's the problem with the theory: **Who are these experts, and how do they know the true market price?**

During the global financial crisis, financial markets collapsed overnight, but EMH theory says if a company was valued at $1 billion at 10 a.m. and one minute later is worth $1, both prices are correct.

The change in price simply reflects new information and is not an error in EMH theory.

FINAL THOUGHTS

Money was created to help us live more easily.

At its core are very basic concepts.

Do not be afraid of your money.

Finance is very simple.

Its ideas are nothing new.

You use the concepts every day without knowing it.

Do not be afraid of your finances.

High Finance is Ordinary Finance!

www.ingramcontent.com/pod-product-compliance
Lightning Source LLC
Chambersburg PA
CBHW051523170526
45165CB00002B/579